Fred's snowman

Fred looked out of the window.
"Oh good," he said. "It's been snowing.
I'm going out into the garden to play.
And then I'm going to make a snowman."

Fred had his breakfast and then he got ready. He put on his hat and coat. He put on his scarf and wellies. He put on his mittens. And then he went out into the garden.

Fred liked the snow.
He jumped up and down in it.
Then he made a snowball and
threw it at the gate.

"Now I'll make my snowman,"
Fred said.
He made a ball of snow. He got more snow and made the snowball bigger and bigger.
"There's his body," Fred said.

"Now I'll make him a head," said Fred.
He made one more big ball of snow.
"There you are, now you have a head."
Fred looked at his snowman.

"Now I'll make his face," said Fred. He made two eyes. He made a nose. He made a mouth. "That's a good face," he said. Fred was very happy with his snowman.

"Now he must have some clothes.
Let me see . . . What does he want?
I know. He wants a hat and coat.
He wants a scarf and wellies.
I'll go and see what I can find."

Fred went back into the house.
"Where can I look for some clothes for my snowman?" he said. "I know, I'll look in here."

Fred found a hat and scarf.
"These will do," he said.
Then he found a coat and some wellies.
"These will do," he said.
And off he went back into the garden.

Kitty, Barney and Lucy were in the kitchen.
"Where's Fred?" said Lucy.

"I don't know," said Barney.
"Is he out playing in the snow?"

"Let's go and see," said Kitty. "I want to go out and play in the snow, too."

“Where’s my new coat? Have you seen my new coat?” said Barney.

“Where are my new hat and scarf? Have you seen my new hat and scarf?” said Kitty.

“And where are my new wellies?” said Lucy. “I can’t find them.”

"FRED!" they said. And they ran into the garden.

"What are you up to, Fred? That's my new coat!" said Barney. "Who said you can have that?"

"And those are my new hat and scarf, too," said Kitty. "Who said you can have them?"

"Oh Fred, these are my new wellies," said Lucy. "You can't have them for your snowman."

Poor Fred. "Look at my snowman!" he said. "He's got no clothes. Now what can I do? I must have something to put on him."

"Well, he can't have my new coat," said Barney.

"And he can't have my new hat and scarf," said Kitty.

"And he can't have my new wellies," said Lucy.

"But he's got no clothes. A snowman must have some clothes," said Fred. "What can I do?"

"Well, I'll let him have my old coat,"
said Barney.

"And I'll let him have my old hat and scarf,"
said Kitty.

"And I'll let him have my old wellies,"
said Lucy.

"That's good. My snowman will like
that," said Fred. "And I know what
I can get him, too."

"What's that?" said Barney.

"It's a secret. You wait and see," said Fred.

"Come on, let's go and get the clothes," said Lucy.
And off they went back into the house.

"Here's my old coat," said Barney.

"And here are my old hat and scarf," said Kitty.

"And here are my old wellies," said Lucy.

"What have you got for your snowman, Fred?"

"It's my trumpet!" said Fred. "I'm going to let my snowman have my trumpet!"

Fred's made a snowman, a snowman, a snowman.
Fred's made a snowman that's looking very good.

I let him have my trumpet, my trumpet, my trumpet.
I let him have my trumpet, that's why he's looking good!

The Snowman
Raymond Briggs